IS OUR MOON THE ONLY MOON IN THE SOLAR SYSTEM?

ASTRONOMY FOR 9 YEAR OLDS CHILDREN'S ASTRONOMY BOOKS

BABY PROFESSOR

EDUCATION KIDS

Speedy Publishing LLC

40 E. Main St. #1156

Newark, DE 19711

www.speedypublishing.com

Copyright 2017

We see the big light in the night sky and call it "the" moon, as if it were the only one. But our solar system has a large number of moons—nobody knows for sure how many. Let's meet some of them.

WHAT MAKES A MOON?

Moons can be smooth and round, jagged, egg-shaped, or in other forms. Most of the moons in our solar system are solid instead of being mainly frozen water or something else, and only a few have atmospheres of their own.

When the solar system formed, 99 percent of its material gathered together into what became our Sun. Some of the other material formed the planets, and what was left went toward the moons and other bodies like asteroids.

SOLAR SYSTEM

SPACE OBJECTS

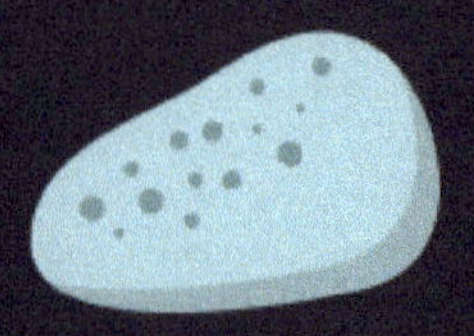

ASTEROID

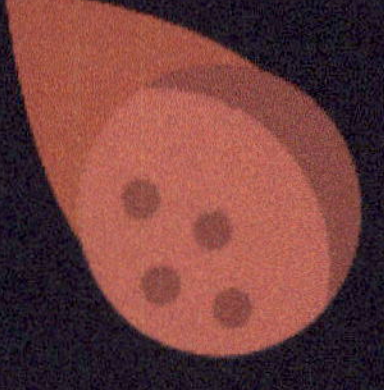

METEORITE

STARS

COMET

W e consider a body a "moon" if it orbits one of the planets. However, some large asteroids also seem to have little asteroids orbiting them as moons, so we may have to update that definition. But even if we just consider moons orbiting planets, we can find hundreds of moons in our solar system!

Most of the planets are named after Greek gods. A lot of the moons are also named after creatures or gods in myths. However, there are exceptions. The moons of Uranus, for instance, are named after fictional characters in plays of Shakespeare and a poem by Alexander Pope.

GREECE

SIMON MARIUS & GALILEO GALILEI

In 1610, both Simon Marius and Galileo Galilei identified four moons in orbit around Jupiter. This discovery also helped confirm that, as the moons orbit the planets, so the planets orbit the Sun.

Asaph Hall in 1877 identified the two moons of Mars: Deimos and Phobos.

S tarting around 2000, humans were able to deploy powerful new telescopes, some orbiting above the atmosphere. This has helped us locate, track, and study dozens of moons around our neighbor planets.

ASTRONOMICAL OBSERVATORY

THE MOONS OF THE SOLAR SYSTEM

Let's start from the Sun and move out past all the planets, to see what moons we find.

SOLAR SYSTEM

Mars
Saturn
Mercury
Earth
Venus
Jupiter
Ura

Mercury and Venus are easy to check off, because they have no moons at all!

EARTH

Our Moon is probably the result of a huge collision. Another body, as big as Mars, collided with Earth. The collision spewed huge amounts of material into space, and much of that material stayed in Earth orbit and eventually came together to form the Moon. This probably happened over four billion years ago, as that is about the age of the oldest rock samples astronauts have brought back from the surface of the Moon.

Scientists call the object that collided with the Earth, Theia. Theia struck so fiercely that it blew parts of itself and the Earth into orbit, and merged the rest of itself with what remained of the original Earth. Theia seems to have had a similar composition to Earth, and this explains why Earth and the surface of the Moon share many characteristics.

As the Moon circles the Earth it slowly rotates so that one side always faces the Earth. The side we can see has huge plains of cooled lava that are evidence of past volcanic activity, while the far side of the Moon does not. Scientists are not sure why the Moon is like this.

Twelve humans have landed on the Moon and then returned to Earth. The first was American astronaut Neil Armstrong in 1969.

MARS

Mars has two moons, Deimos and Phobos. They have circular orbits around the equator of Mars, but they themselves are irregularly shaped. Phobos is slowly losing altitude, and in 40 million years or so will either break apart under the pull of Mars' gravity, creating a ring around Mars, or crash into the planet.

JUPITER

Jupiter, the first gas giant in the Solar System, has more than fifty moons. Most of the moons orbit in the same direction as Jupiter rotates, but a few orbit in the opposite direction. These tend to be moons whose orbits are not round, but more of a deep ellipse.

G anymede, one of Jupiter's moons, is the largest moon in our solar system, and is even bigger than the planet Mercury. Ganymede is one of the four "Galilean moons" that Galileo and Simon Marius discovered in 1610. The others are:

- Io: it has the most volcanic activity of any planetary body in the solar system.

- Europa: this moon may have a huge global ocean of water underneath its crust

Callisto: Callisto also may have an ocean of water under its surface.

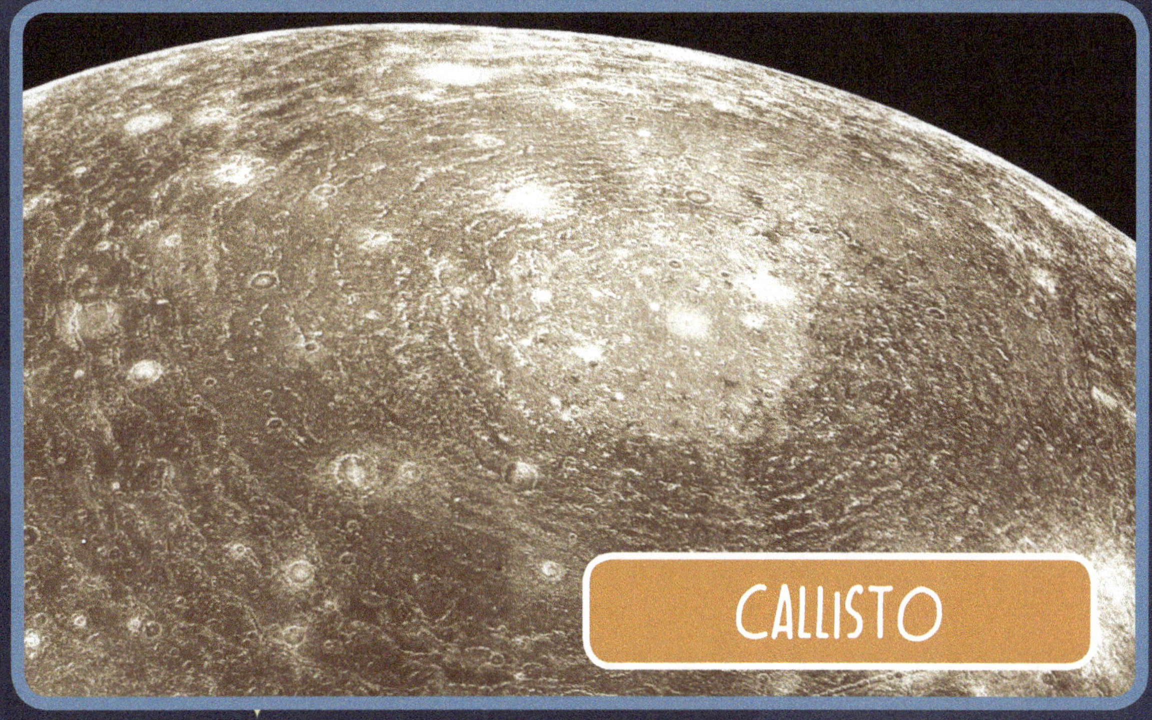

SATURN

Saturn also has more than fifty moons (the number keeps growing as better and better scientific equipment provides new discoveries). Saturn also has famous rings, made up of particles as small as dust and as large as small asteroids. There are also some "shepherd moons" whose orbits align with the rings and help keep the rings organized.

SATURN

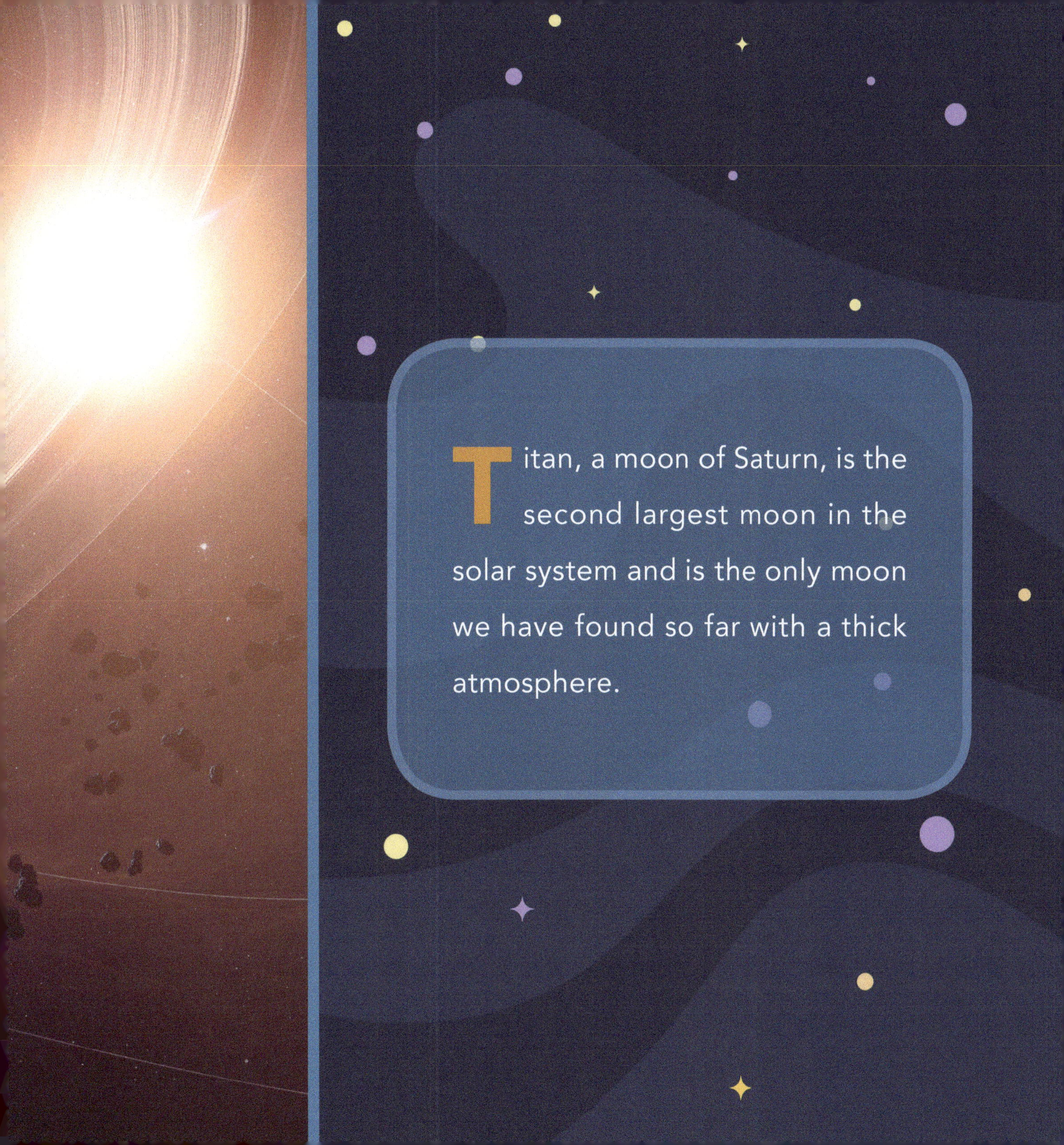

Titan, a moon of Saturn, is the second largest moon in the solar system and is the only moon we have found so far with a thick atmosphere.

Enceladus is only one-tenth the size of Titan, but it has intriguing features. It regularly vents plumes of water vapor into space, and scientists speculate that under its crust is a deep ocean of water circling the moon. Since scientists have also detected indications of hydrothermal (hot water) activity, and since warm water is essential for the creation of life as we now know it, it is possible that conditions might be right in that ocean to support the creation of life.

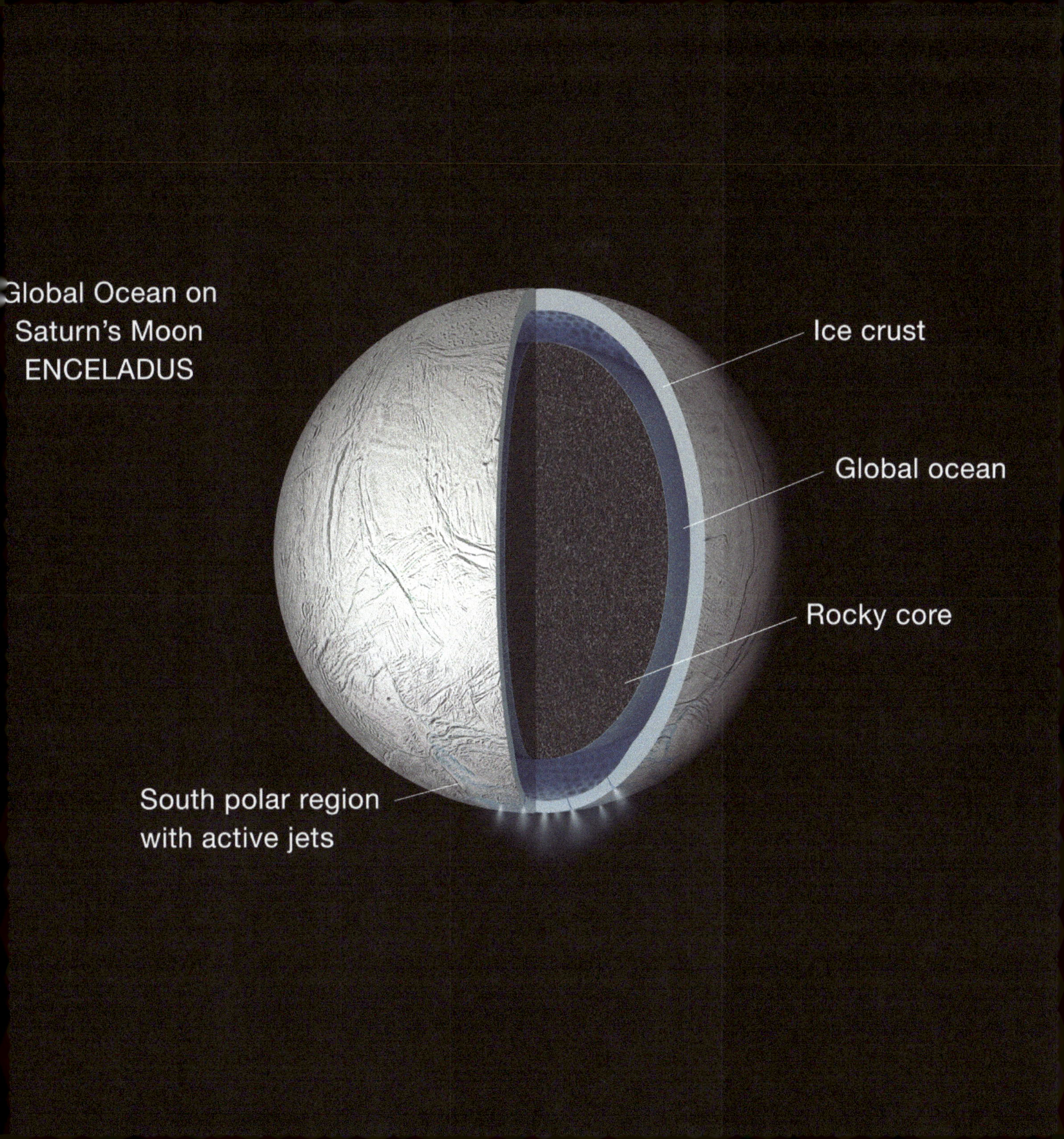

Global Ocean on
Saturn's Moon
ENCELADUS
Ice crust
Global ocean
Rocky core
South polar region
with active jets

Mimas is the smallest body in the solar system with enough mass to allow it to form into an approximate sphere. It looks sort of like the Death Star from the Star Wars movies, but the round place where the death ray should come from is an impact crater that is about 80 miles in diameter.

apetus is visually striking, with one light-colored side and one darker side. This may be caused by migration together of darker materials which absorb more sunlight and are therefore warmer than the lighter surface areas.

URANUS

So far, we have found 27 moons around Uranus. Most of the moons near the planet seem to be about half rock and half water ice. Miranda may be the most interesting of the moons of Uranus. It has a craggy, broken surface that looks like the moon was involved in collisions with many other small moons or large asteroids.

SHAKESPEARE'S PLAY

Most of the moons of Uranus are named after characters in Shakespeare's plays. Most of the moons, like Titania, are also a soft gray color.

NEPTUNE

Neptune has at least 13 moons. The largest is Triton. It is as large as Pluto, which is a dwarf planet with an orbit further out than Neptune's. Triton orbits Neptune in the opposite direction to the planet's rotation, and it may have been a wandering body from the outer edges of the solar system that became trapped by Neptune's gravitational field. That area is called the Kuiper Belt, and is home to millions of comets, asteroids, and proto-planets of many sizes. Some of the Kuiper Belt objects are as big as the moons we know and have named!

Triton has a unique bumpy surface that may have been caused by Neptune's gravitational forces, or may be a relic of its earlier history when it was still a wandering object.

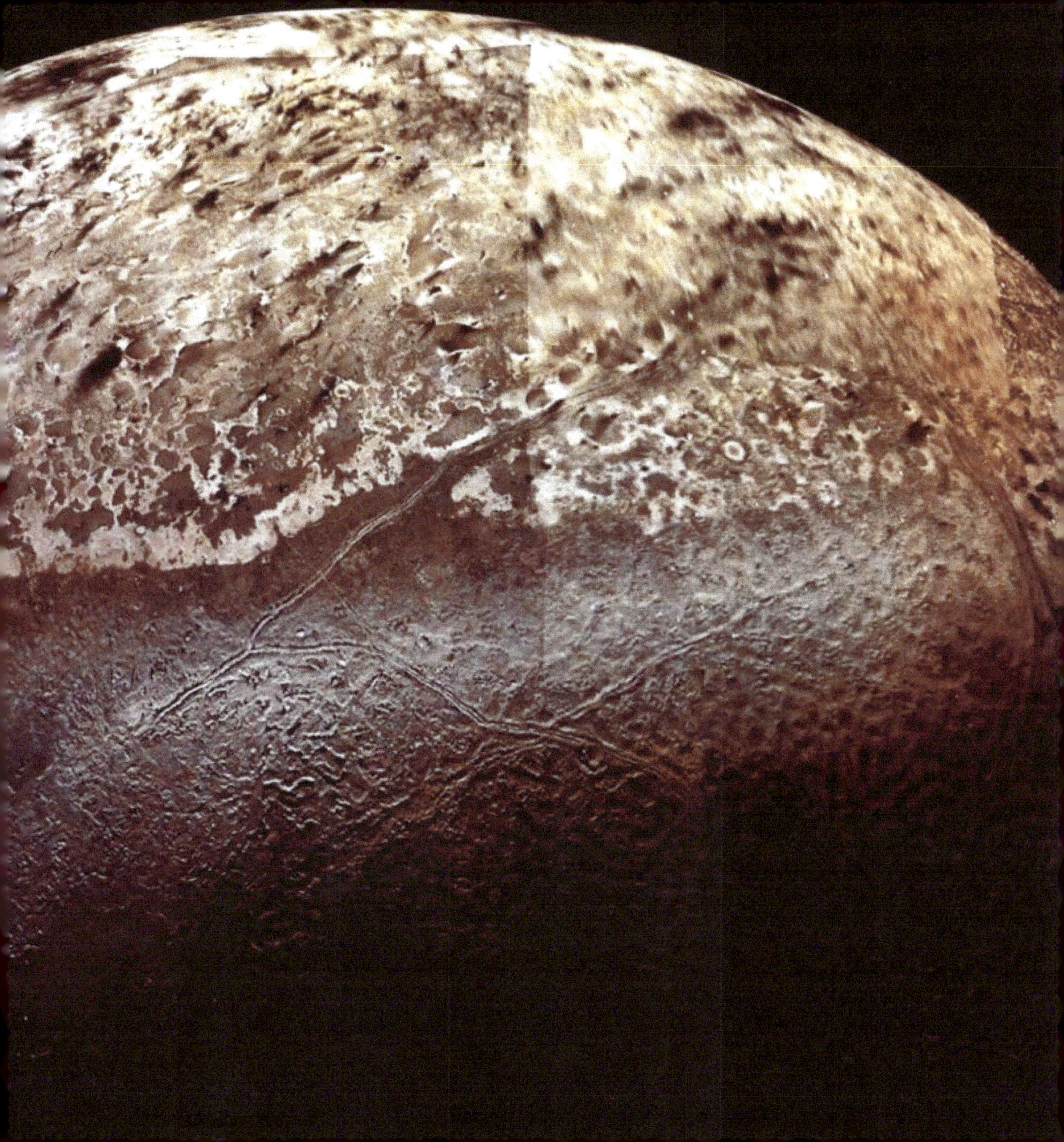

OTHER MOONS

We mentioned Pluto, which is no longer considered a planet. But it is still part of the solar system! And it has such an odd arrangement of moons that it is worth studying.

Pluto's largest moon is called Charon. It is about half the size of Pluto, and may have formed the way our Moon formed, after some object collided with the planet it now orbits. Pluto and Charon pull on each other so hard that, while the moon goes around the dwarf planet, the pair of them also orbit a point in space called a barycenter. They are more like twin moons with no central planet than a planet with a moon!

Charon has no atmosphere, but it has a complex geologic history. Images and scans from a satellite fly-past revealed mountains, landslides and deep canyons marking the surface of the moon.

PLUTO & CHARON

n 2005 scientists found two more moons of Pluto. They are tiny, and are called Nix and Hydra—and they also orbit the barycenter at a great distance.

Beyond Pluto is Eris, a dwarf planet with a moon of its own, Dysnomia. Even further out is the dwarf planet Haumea, with at least two moons: Hi'iaka and Namaka.

ERIS

REACHING THE MOONS

Many groups are working out how humans can leave the Earth and start colonies on other planets or moons in our solar system. Moons like Enceladus, which may have water available, are interesting candidates. These projects will need volunteers if they ever happen, and you may have a chance to think about going into space. To understand more about what's involved, read Baby Professor books like Sally Ride: First American Woman in Space, What is an Astronaut? and The Unfortunate Launch of the Space Shuttle Challenger.

Visit

BABY PROFESSOR
EDUCATION KIDS

www.BabyProfessorBooks.com
to download Free Baby Professor eBooks
and view our catalog of new and exciting
Children's Books